10/1/02
Barner + Noble . com
$17.25

Santa Fe Community

D0803280

DATE DUE

	MAR 0 9 2005			

DEMC

The Ancient Splendor of Prehistoric Cahokia

The Ancient Splendor of Prehistoric Cahokia

By

Sidney Denny, Ph.D.

and

Ernest L. Schusky, Ph.D.

Illustrated by

John Adkins Richardson

Ozark Publishing, Inc.
P.O. Box 228
Prairie Grove, AR 72753

Santa Fe Community
College Library
6401 Richards Ave.
Santa Fe, NM 87508

Library of Congress cataloging-in-publication data

Denny, Sidney G.
   The ancient splendor of prehistoric Cahokia / by
Sidney Denny and Ernest L. Schusky ; illustrated by
John Adkins Richardson. — 2nd ed.
       p.   cm.
   Includes bibliographical references.
   ISBN 1-56763-271-8 (cloth : alk. paper). —
ISBN 1-56763-272-6 (paper : alk. paper)
   1. Cahokia Site (East Saint Louis, Ill.) 2.
Mississippian culture—Illinois. 3. Illinois—
Antiquities. I. Schusky, Ernest Lester, 1931- . II.
Richardson, John Adkins. III. Title.
E99.M6815D45 1997
977.3'89—dc20   96-32662
                                              CIP

Copyright © 1997 by Sidney Denny and Ernest L. Schusky

All rights reserved

Printed in the United States of America

To members of the Cahokian Society
and all others who have helped unlock
the mysteries of Cahokia

Monks Mound (so called because in the nineteenth century the Trappist Order established a monastery here), Cahokia, Illinois

Conical and Flattop Mounds on South Plaza, Cahokia

NOTE:
A list of illustrations within the text appears on page 38

1

Cahokia's Place in Prehistory

The Cahokia Mounds site represents the most complex social and political culture of prehistoric North American Indians. The people at this site lived in such a diverse society, with everyone doing so many different things, that Cahokia deserves to be described as a city.

For centuries, Cahokia was the urban center for Indians as far away as the Canadian border, the Gulf of Mexico, and the Appalachian Mountains. About forty thousand people lived in the city itself, but hundreds of thousands of Indians were affected by Cahokian developments.

Archaeologists did little work at Cahokia before 1960 because the site was so large and complex. However, with help from the National Science Foundation, scientists determined the site was unique. It was not only the focus of all Indian life in the Mississippi Valley, but also it was the only urban center to occur in North America before the arrival of Europeans and Africans.

THE ANCIENT SPLENDOR OF CAHOKIA

The Cahokia Mounds lie along the Mississippi River, the remnants of a prehistoric city whose splendor started more than a thousand years ago. The mounds remained a mystery because of prejudice in the dominant society. Many people refused to believe

Indians were capable of achieving and executing such complex architectural skills as are reflected in the mounds. Thus, one early account claims the mound builders were a lost tribe of Israel; another attributes the mounds to a wandering band of Welsh explorers.

Today, anthropologists know Indians built Cahokia and many other mounds more than five hundred years before Columbus found the New World. Yet, many mysteries remain. Undoubtedly, the architects of the mounds were influenced by an urban style of life that first began among the Mayan in the Yucatan Peninsula and became well established in the Valley of Mexico by A.D. 300.

Did southern colonizers from Mexico bring their ideas and way of life to the Mississippi Valley? Or was the exchange limited to a few ideas spread by a handful of travelers? Did the Cahokian development parallel the Mexican development with only limited contact between the two areas? These questions are the modern mystery of Cahokia.

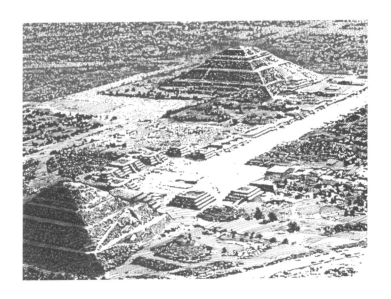

THE PREHISTORIC BASE FOR
CAHOKIAN CULTURE

About thirty-five hundred years ago in the lower part of the Mississippi Valley, hunting and gathering peoples, or food collectors, began to plant and cultivate squash and gourds. While most of their food came from collecting, these Indians laid a base for agriculture.

Their experimentation in food production led to agriculture. The ancient focus on plants, such as squash, established myths about its origin and gave the women who attended the plants an important place in religion. The distinct way of life for this time period is called Late Archaic.

The Late Archaic lifestyle is best illustrated by an archaeological site called Poverty Point. This site is close to Vicksburg, Mississippi.

Six large, concentric ridges about four thousand feet across, shaped like octagons with the long sides curved, surrounded a conical mound and some other small prominences. Although houses were built on top of the nearly twelve miles of mounds, the total complex suggests religious and political purposes. The architecture, some female figurines, and green celts, possibly imitating jade, led the archaeologists who excavated the site to believe that Olmecs, a people from the Gulf Coast of Mexico, influenced the beginning of Late Archaic culture.

However, the site contains very little pottery,

which seems odd if Olmecs initiated Late Archaic. Most important, no evidence exists for planting or using corn. Modern anthropologists think that Olmecs surely would have introduced corn if many of them moved to the Mississippi Valley.

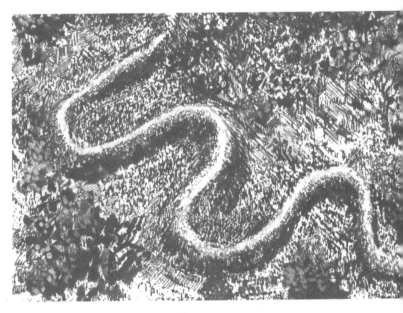

THE SPREAD OF CULTURE DURING MIDDLE WOODLAND

Several centuries after the Poverty Point culture, new religious ideas about the proper form of burial spread through the Mississippi, Missouri, Arkansas, and Ohio River Valleys. Indians spent considerable effort in constructing burial mounds. Log or stone vaults were covered with earth to form rectangular or conical mounds.

People also built mounds in the shape of animals; these structures were known as effigy mounds. Another shape was conical. In this period conical mounds covered cremations or burials in log chambers. The dead who received such attention obviously were honored people because of the grave goods as well as construction of the mound. Possibly, they were political

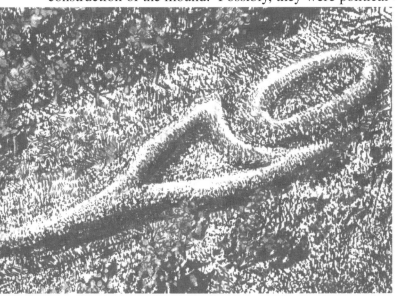

figures; more likely they were the elders of a descent group or clan who combined religious and political power with kinship.

The customs that characterized this Middle Woodland stage persisted until nearly A.D. 400. For subsistence, people continued to cultivate squash and gourds, which were first domesticated in Mexico. Few other Mexican traits appear in the Midwest of North America during the Middle Woodland. In addition to squash and gourds, native crops, such as the sunflower, were cultivated to provide most of the plant food.

The rest of the food supply was obtained by hunting and fishing. Wild game was especially important in late winter and early spring.

All these developments in the third and fourth centuries laid the foundation for the growth of a remarkable trade network throughout the Midwest. The exchange of goods and ideas led to the flowering of Middle Woodland culture, with its center at Cahokia.

MIDDLE WOODLAND LIFE

In the period between 200 B.C. and A.D. 400 the Ohio and Illinois River Valleys witnessed an unusual flow of luxury goods into their areas. No large towns existed, but communities strung along a river valley were organized by political leaders; they may have been clan elders or individuals who excelled at trade.

These leaders were able to organize labor for the construction of large effigy mounds, geometric embankments, and conical burial mounds. Archaeologists know much about the widespread trade networks because many exotic goods were buried with some of the dead. The wealthy burials suggest the beginnings of social classes, but social stratification was unusual in North America. Ideas of high standing, or ranking, may have come from Mexico, but no solid evidence of such influence is found. If social classes were formed, they disappeared by the time EuroAmericans came to the Midwest.

A number of the sites suggest that hereditary chiefs concentrated wealth, winning power by bestow-ing their wealth on followers. Another possibility is that enterprising individuals built up wealth by exchange in long-distance trips. They, too, would gain prestige by giving away wealth to friends and neigh-bors, not by accumulating it. The wealth of grave

11

goods often consists of gifts being bestowed on the deceased.

Giveaways continued to be practiced by most North American Indians. In Middle Woodland sites, the prestige gained by giving away wealth was dis-

played by symbols of hawks, snakes, deer, and other animals. Skilled artisans carved these symbols in materials such as raw copper or mica, a rock-like mineral of various colors that can be separated into thin sheets. Such artwork is unique to prehistoric times.

THE TRANSITION FROM MIDDLE WOOD-LAND TO CAHOKIA

After A.D. 500 the Midwest experienced cooler weather, which affected the growing season. Perhaps the short season led to decreased population. Whatever the reason, the impressive effigy mounds ceased to be built. In some places people devoted their energy to building defensive mounds at inaccessible sites. The most impressive of these sites is at Fort Ancient, near Cincinnati, Ohio.

In southern North America, the earlier traditions persisted. Southern artists continued fine work in copper and other rare materials. Conical burial mounds are found near towns. Elsewhere, people built truncated pyramids, ones without the top peak of the pyramid. Temples were likely built on top.

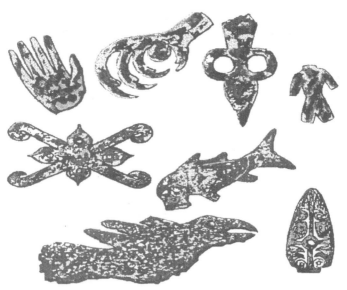

Warmer weather returned to the Midwest about A.D. 750. The effects of this climatic change are uncertain, but by A.D. 800 corn from Mexico was added to the previously borrowed squash and gourds. Sunflowers, amaranth, and other native plants continued to be farmed.

As years passed, people learned to cultivate corn intensively, and it became a basic part of the diet. Intensive agriculture at the mouths of the Missouri, Illinois, and Ohio Rivers laid the basis for growth of Cahokia. The intensive agriculture was necessary to support the dense population that grew at the site. However, Cahokia's strategic location was most important in determining its development into a city.

THE CAHOKIA MOUNDS COMPLEX

Urban Cahokia was the heart of a larger complex lining the American Bottoms. Related towns are found six miles north and twelve miles south. More mounds and dwellings stretched westward into what is now East St. Louis and across the river in St. Louis,

Missouri. Cahokia, itself, consisted of more than one hundred mounds, covering six square miles. The mounds vary in shape, from conical to truncated. The larger mounds surround a plaza, the size of six football fields. A wooden stockade encircled the plaza and inner mounds.

MONKS MOUND IN THE CAHOKIAN COMPLEX

At the north end of the Cahokian plaza, Monks Mound rises one hundred feet to dominate both site and plaza. Its fifteen-acre base makes it the largest in North America except for Teotihuacan near Mexico City and Cholula, near Puebla. Both of these sites are in the Valley of Mexico more than a thousand miles from Cahokia. Some ideas must have passed between

the two valleys, but the growth at Cahokia was largely
a parallel, rather than a borrowing, of what happened
in the south. Whereas the Mexican pyramids are built
of a stone exterior filled with rubble, Cahokia was built
entirely of earth, taken basketful by basketful from
borrow pits south of the plaza. After taking earth from
the pits, the holes were later filled in and carefully
sealed over.

Archaeologists have traced fourteen stages of construction, which result in a large terrace at front, a second terrace on the east, and two levels on top. This truncated top suggests the upper terrace was used for a large ceremonial building with ritual, such as dancing, performed before it on the slightly lower terrace. Archaeological excavation of the top terrace located post pits that seem to be the remains of a large temple, but evidence is insufficient to prove the building's purpose.

MOUND 72: SOCIAL SPLENDOR OF THE CITY

Although Monks Mound dominates the site physically, a six-foot-high, inconspicuous ridge mound a short distance south of the plaza has revealed the most about Cahokian prehistory, while raising a host of perplexing questions. This feature is known simply as Mound 72.

No one paid much attention to Mound 72 until the mid-1960s. One winter Dr. Melvin Fowler pored over a map of Cahokia. He discovered Mound 72 lay on a major east-west axis which intersected another major axis, running north and south. These axes were determined by the remains of large post pits which seem to have contained boundary markers.

The next summer Fowler dug at the axes inter-
section, discovering the remains of a large post pit. A
pole three feet in diameter had been sunk eight feet
into the ground. The pole had been removed by the
Cahokians, but they left smaller crib posts intact.
Evidence of the larger pole remained in a slightly different color of soil. The wooden remains of the crib
posts were dated by the Carbon 14 remaining.
(Carbon 14 is absorbed by all living things. At death
the Carbon 14 disintegrates at a regular rate.) The
Carbon 14 from the crib posts yields a date of A.D.
950.

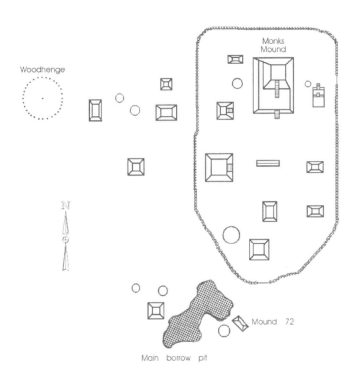

Woodhenge

Monks
Mound

N

Mound 72

Main borrow pit

POLITICS AND RELIGION RECONSTRUCTED FROM MOUND 72

Near the post pit, Fowler discovered the skeleton of an older male lying on a shell platform, actually all that remained of a cape to which shells had been attached.

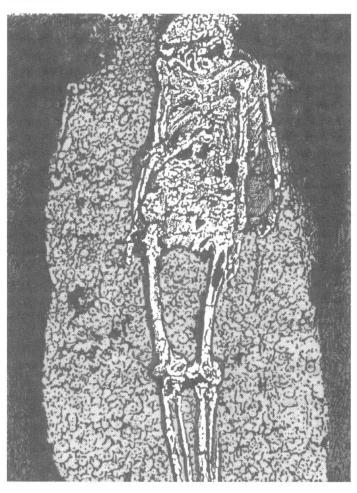

Alongside his burial were a tribute bundle of three hundred finely chipped, never used arrowheads, and another one of four hundred points. They were all that remained of quivers filled with arrows at the time of burial. Other buried wealth consisted of a roll of raw copper, several bushels of mica, and nineteen chunkey stones. (Chunkey stones are disks with concave holes on both sides. They seem to have been used in games of a ritual nature.)

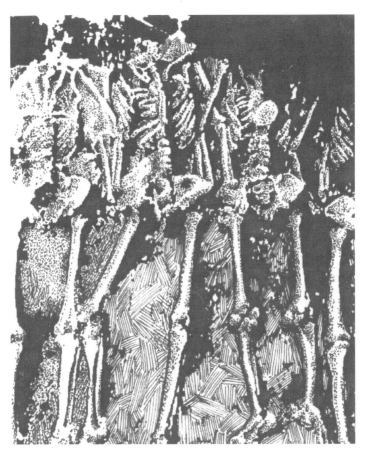

Four other skeletons of adult males suggest retainers were killed to accompany their leader. Further in the mound, Fowler's team discovered the skeletons of fifty-three young women, who also must have been sacrificed to accompany their leader in death, perhaps being drugged before death. Such a practice was common in Mexico.

Human sacrifices strongly suggest that Mexican ideas were being spread to Cahokia. Fifty-two sacrificial victims would have confirmed such influence, because that number is sacred in Mayan and Aztec ritual. But why fifty-three? Was there some scant knowledge of Mexican practices, but a deliberate rejection of details, or did the Cahokians make a reinterpretation? Or could the number of women sacrificed have been coincidental? The idea of human sacrifice at death has occurred to many peoples. Perhaps the Cahokians invented the practice independently.

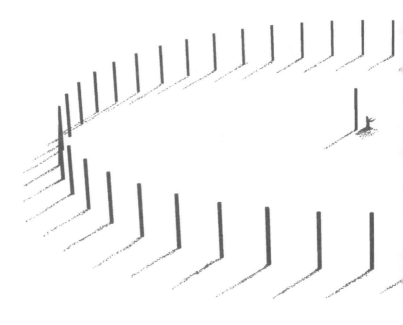

WOODHENGE: CAHOKIA'S CALENDAR

For years archaeologists were mystified that no calendars occurred north of Mexico, because astronomical knowledge was important to the Mexicans. When anthropologists thought Mexican influence was powerful, the idea of the year should have spread northward. Yet, until 1960, the search for calendric knowledge was fruitless. But in 1961 archaeologists discovered four circular constructions at Cahokia, measuring the sun's solstices, its rising and setting farthest to the north in the summer and farthest to the south in the winter.

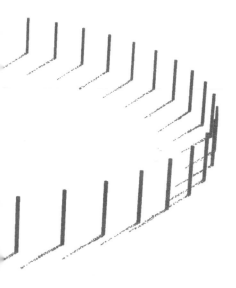

Dr. Warren Wittry, working one thousand yards west of Monks Mound, unearthed a series of post pits that he first termed "bathtubs." Later work confirmed the pits formed a four-hundred-foot circle of forty-eight poles, with a center pole five feet east of the true center. Archaeologists had found the first of several calendars.

Wittry nicknamed the remains "Woodhenge." Many scientists felt he had proved a powerful Mexican influence. However, another recently discovered site, called Sunwatch, near Dayton, Ohio, shows an even earlier and simpler yearly measure. At Sunwatch, the markers determine the frost-free seasons, rather than equinoxes and solstices.

At Cahokia, why weren't there fifty-two posts in the circle if Mexican knowledge was fundamental? The number, forty-eight, suggests a parallel or independent development. Why wouldn't agricultural people determine frost-free seasons on the basis of sunrises? Wouldn't the next step be to determine equinoxes and solstices?

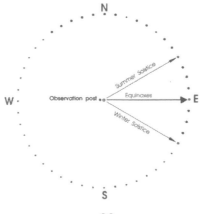

MEASURING THE YEAR

Wittry calculates that from the central observation post of Woodhenge, an observer would see the sun rise exactly over the eastern post at the spring and fall equinoxes. The fourth pole north of the post marks the summer solstice. An observer would see the sun rise over the fourth pole south at the winter solstice. Members of the contemporary Cahokian Society gather at the reconstructed Woodhenge to observe and celebrate these dates.

For the study of prehistory, Wittry's discovery of Woodhenge confirmed what anthropologists expected of cultural processes. Some basic elements of Mexican religion filtered to the north, but Mississippian peoples added many features of their own to what they borrowed. Thus, independent invention is impressive at Cahokia, and doubtless, Mexican anthropologists eventually will find Cahokian ideas that filtered to Mexico. Borrowing or diffusion is rarely a one-way process. Just as Indians have borrowed much from the larger society around them, they have given much to it. For example, if Indians had not taught the early settlers in New England how to raise corn and beans, the Europeans would have starved, for their agricultural methods failed in the New World.

POLITICAL AND ECONOMIC LIFE AT CAHOKIA

What seems to distinguish Cahokian society from Mexico most is social organization. North American Indians are equalitarian and democratic, in contrast to the socially stratified Aztecs and their predecessors. It is clear that individual Cahokians were becoming ranked by differences in wealth, but there is no evidence for specialized traders and artisans who formed the social classes that arose in Mexico.

Instead, evidence points to the growing power of chiefs who directed a flow of wealth. While much wealth came up to the chiefs, they only retained power if they redistributed this wealth back down to followers.

Thus, the riches in grave goods, such as copper and arrows, were final gifts from followers, including gifts from allied distant tribes. While such exchange of wealth over wide areas is interpreted as trade, it is better understood as gift-giving or reciprocity.

In reciprocal gift-giving people give away what they do best. These gifts obligate recipients to return gifts of similar value—their best art and crafts. Such exchange resembles trade, but it lacks a profit motive. The exchange does not result in notable accumulations of wealth among families.

The flow of goods from Cahokia to most of eastern North America was largely a result of social and political factors, but since the exchange involved production and distribution of goods, it must also be considered economic. Such organization contrasts with Mexico, where specialized traders operated on a profit motive that caused striking concentrations of wealth and the development of rigidly separated social classes.

THE UNIQUENESS OF CAHOKIA

Cahokia was not only the earliest urban site north of Mexico, but also the only one to exist before arrival of peoples from the Old World. Archaeologists see Cahokian origins as arising in the upper reaches of the Ohio Valley, whose peoples built burial and effigy mounds, intensified agriculture with both native species and a few borrowed from Mexico, and built an exchange network that reached from the Rocky Mountains eastward to the Appalachians and from the Great Lakes south to the Gulf of Mexico.

The native peoples at Cahokia expanded upon this social and economic organization after A.D. 800. Political power focused in chiefdoms, though chiefs lived a material life much like other people. They did have unusual political power compared with modern Indians. This power came from giving away wealth, not only to other Cahokians, but also to other tribes throughout the eastern two-thirds of the continent.

Although some ideas diffused to the Cahokians

from Mexico, their society became distinct, developing its own traits and style, expanding in a unique way. Between A.D. 800 and A.D. 1200 Cahokia would have seemed the center of the universe to most Native Americans between the Appalachian and Rocky Mountains.

Yet, the site remains mysterious to present-day peoples in many ways. Why it ended is as much a puzzle as how it began. Even the descendants of the Cahokians are unknown. Common sense suggests that the Cahokian descendants are Illinois Indians or other Algonquian peoples living in the Midwest at time of contact with EuroAmericans. On the other hand, Siouan-speaking peoples, now living in the Missouri Valley, share more traits with prehistoric Cahokia. They also have a complex social organization such as must have existed at Cahokia, and their legends speak of origins in the Cahokia area.

Archaeologist continue to chip away at the mysteries. They have proved beyond doubt the city was built by American Indians. They are showing it was much less dependent on Mexican ideas than previously thought, and they are demonstrating a complexity of culture that destroys earlier white stereotypes of "primitive" Indians. It is left for future generations of archaeologists to determine Cahokia's origins and why its urban way of life came to an end.

37

LIST OF ILLUSTRATIONS

Pages

OTHER BOOKS TO READ

For Young Readers

Jane Chisholm. *Living in Prehistoric Times*. London: Usborne Publishing, 1982. A good introduction to world prehistoric times, with excellent illustrations for the young reader.

Dennis Fradin. *Archaeology*. Chicago: Children's Press, 1983. An excellent introduction to the purpose of archaeology, showing how professionals work and what their goals are.

Various Contributors. *Cahokia: City of the Sun*. Collinsville, Illinois: Cahokia Mounds Museum Society, 1992. A well-written and photo-illustrated, comprehensive overview of Cahokia Mounds, for readers of all ages.

For Young Adults

Kathleen King. *Cricket Sings: A Novel of PreColumbia Cahokia*. Athens, Ohio: Ohio University

Press, 1983. A novel for the young adult and adult reader, reconstructing life at Cahokia as the author interprets it.

George Stuart. "Who Were the Mound Builders?" *National Geographic*. Vol. 142, No. 6 (December 1972): 782–801. Extensively illustrated with photographs and artists' reconstruction.

For Adult Readers

Greater St. Louis Archaeological Society of St. Louis. *Cahokia Brought to Life*. St. Louis, Missouri: Author, 1989.

Melvin Fowler. *The Cahokia Atlas*. Springfield, Illinois: Studies in Illinois Archaeology, No. 6, 1989.

Melvin Fowler. "A Precolumbian Urban Center on the Mississippi." *Scientific Amercian*, 233:2 (August, 1975): 93–101.

Mikels Skele. *The Great Knob: Interpretations of Monks Mound*. Springfield, Illinois: Historic Preservation Society, No. 4, 1988.

Santa Fe Community
College Library
6401 Richards Ave.
Santa Fe, NM 8750ₑ